VERMONT CENTER FOR ECOSTUDIES
UNITING PEOPLE & SCIENCE FOR CONSERVATION

Northeast Temperate Network
Inventory & Monitoring Program

Breeding Landbird Monitoring Program

© Bryan Pfeiffer

VOLUNTEER TRAINING MANUAL

VOLUNTEER TRAINING MANUAL

Contents

Figures

Tables

Inventory & Monitoring Program

BREEDING LANDBIRD MONITORING PROGRAM

Background

Birds are an important component of park ecosystems – their high body temperature, rapid metabolism, and high ecological position in most food webs make them a good indicator of local and regional ecosystem change. Among the public, birds are a high profile taxa, and many parks provide information on the status and trends of the park's avian community through their interpretive materials and programs.

In developing comprehensive long-term monitoring plans, landbirds (a general term used to describe relatively small, terrestrial birds, excluding raptors and upland game birds) are among the best taxonomic groups to monitor because: 1) they are the most easily and inexpensively detected and identified vertebrate animals, 2) a single survey method is effective for many species, 3) accounting and managing for many species with different ecological requirements promotes conservation strategies at the landscape scale, 4) many reference datasets and standard methods are available, and 5) the response variability is fairly well understood.

In addition, birds are a useful biotic indicator of the effects of habitat fragmentation, an ecological stressor that all Northeast Temperate Network (NETN) parks are impacted by. Gaining insights into the long-term trends of avian species composition and relative abundance will provide one measure for assessing the ecological integrity and sustainability of northeastern temperate systems.

This training manual provides guidance to volunteer observers participating in the Northeast Temperate Network's (NETN) breeding landbird monitoring. In addition to providing an overview of study design, details on are provided on survey procedures, training exercises, and data management responsibilities.

Goals and Objectives

The overall goal of this program is to monitor the status and trends of breeding landbird populations, to assess changes in ecological integrity and the impacts of key stressors, and to guide management decisions affecting avian populations and other natural resources. The specific objectives of this protocol are to: 1) Determine annual changes in species composition and relative abundance of bird species during the breeding season; 2) Improve our understanding of the relationships between breeding birds and habitat; and 3) improve our understanding of the effects that management actions, such as silvicultural practices and mowing regimes, have on bird populations by correlating changes in bird communities with changes in specific habitat variables.

Sampling Design

Numerous sampling approaches have been used to quantify the status and trends of bird populations, and many different monitoring programs are currently in place throughout North America to determine local, regional, or national trends in bird numbers. Most survey methods allow simultaneous collection of information about species that share a common life history or habitat type, but no single method will adequately sample either the diversity of habitats that birds occupy, or life history groups such as seabirds, songbirds, raptors, and shorebirds.

The sampling design used for this program involves a series of sampling stations laid out on a systematic grid that are sampled during 10-minute point counts. For landbirds, point counts are the most widely used quantitative method of monitoring bird populations. This technique involves using a standardized methodology to record all birds seen or heard during a fixed amount of time at many widely spaced count locations. For each bird observed, the time (minute of the count) and distance band (0-10 m, 10-25 m, 25-50 m, and >50 m) will be recorded. The methodology is largely based on songbird monitoring protocols developed for the Lower Mississippi Valley Joint Venture.

Within most parks there will be multiple study sites consisting of between 5 and 10 sampling points, called point count stations, spaced between 200 and 250 m apart. On a given survey date, each station is sampled for 10 minutes. Each observer will receive a map along with detailed instructions on how to reach the study site and locate each station. GPS coordinates will also be provided for each point. All point count stations will be marked with a small metal tree tag inscribed with, for example, "SH #1" (indicating Point 1 at the Sugar Hollow study site), as well as blue flagging tape, clearly marked with the same information.

Each observer should conduct a pre-survey visit to become familiar with his/her site. It is _essential_ that observers bring with them a hand compass and know how to use it (see Appendix 2), as bearings between stations may change due to topographic obstacles, wetlands, or simply to coincide with the most suitable habitat. Unless noted otherwise, all bearings on the site directions sheets are _magnetic_, not true (so do not correct the declination on your compass – **but check your directions to be sure!**).

Survey Assumptions

The data being collected during point counts will be analyzed with two different methods (distance sampling and removal models), each of which is an independent approach to estimating the probability of detecting an individual. If we can accurately estimate this probability, we can estimate the number of birds that were NOT seen or heard during the point count, and derive a better estimate of bird abundance than we would get using only birds actually seen or heard. It is important to understand the assumptions of these methods, and to work to meet them. Both approaches assume that birds are correctly identified to species, and that each individual is only recorded once. The distance sampling approach further assumes that all birds within 10 meters of the observer (the first distance band) are always detected, and that the distance band recorded is the correct band. The removal modeling approach assumes that the time recorded for the individual bird is the time it was first heard or seen, and that observers are equally likely to hear a bird of a given species during every minute (e.g., the observer is just as likely to hear or see a Brown Creeper at minute one as he or she is at minute five).

When observers are collecting data, they should keep in mind that the most important assumptions are that **birds are correctly identified to species**, and that **each individual is recorded only once**. The next most important assumptions are that **all birds close to you (within 10 meters) are recorded**, and that **distance estimates are correct**. The removal modeling assumptions are less important, and all other data that are collected (e.g., nest location, and whether the bird is singing, calling, or seen) are secondary to the primary goals of getting accurate species and distance information. If observers feel that they are unable to meet the assumptions of the distance sampling or the removal modeling approaches, they should provide a written comment with as much detail as possible when they submit their data forms. This will be a tremendous help to the data analysis phase of the project!

Observer Training: Estimating Distances to Birds Seen or Heard

As mentioned above, the most critical aspects of this monitoring program are to ensure that species are identified correctly and that double-counting individual birds is avoided. In addition, in order to estimate the abundance of birds within study plots, it is important that observers accurately estimate distances to detected birds. Practice can greatly improve observers' ability to correctly estimate distances. Participants should read through both the self-administered distance training exercises found in this section and the survey procedures described in the following section, and then practice distance estimation in a habitat similar to the one in which they will be surveying birds. All observers should "recalibrate" themselves by practicing these training exercises at the beginning of each field season.

1. In a habitat similar to the one in which you will be conducting point counts, begin by placing flagging at 10 m, 25 m and 50 m from a marked central point (e.g., the point count station). To do this, volunteers can either use a 25 m (or longer) tape measure, a measured length of rope, or estimate by measuring the length of their walking pace.

2. Remove the markers set up in step 1, and then walk around the "study site" placing flagging at four or five locations visible from the station. Return to the central point and estimate the distance band (e.g., 0-10m, 10-25m, 25-50m, >50m) that each flag falls within, recording them in a field book. Then, using a measuring device or pacing, measure the distance to each flag and compare your initial estimate to the actual distance. Repeat this exercise several times until you can consistently estimate distances.

3. The majority of birds are usually heard but not seen, and estimating distances to birds that are only heard is often the greatest source of error in VCP counts. Standing at the central point of your "point count station", listen for vocalizing birds. Choose one consistently vocalizing individual and estimate the distance band in which it is singing. Remember, the horizontal distance should be estimated, as if a plumb-bob was lowered to the ground from the bird's location. Try to visually identify the tree or branch where you think the bird is, and estimate the horizontal distance to an object that can be seen directly below where you think the bird is vocalizing from. Now, walk toward the vocalizing bird until you can either see it or accurately estimate its location. Using your measuring device or pacing, walk back to the point count station and compare your initial estimate to the actual distance. Repeat this exercise for several birds at various distances.

Note: These training exercises can be accomplished more quickly with the help of an assistant.

Survey Procedures

1. **Navigate to Point.** Use a GPS or map and compass to navigate to your points. The forest routes have been marked with blue flagging every 25 to 100 m (depending on the density of the vegetation). If any of the flagging is worn out, please collect it and replace it with fresh flagging. See Appendix B for tips on navigating with map and compass.

2. **Count Conditions.** Counts should be conducted early in the morning and during proper survey conditions. We recommend a 0500 hrs start time. Winds should be calm to light (< 7 mph; Code 2 or less on the Beaufort Scale, Table 1). Acceptable weather conditions for counting birds include a sky condition of 5 or less (although fog should not interfere with visual identification of birds; Table 2). Clear conditions or slightly damp are ideal. Counts should not be conducted in rain, unless it is very light. <u>The rule is to conduct surveys only in weather that is unlikely to reduce count numbers</u>. Generally, the more calm and clear the weather, the better the count. It is advisable to listen to the forecast the night before the survey and plan accordingly.

Prior to the first point count, fill in the site name, date, and observer name on the field mapping card (Figure 1). Then, upon arriving at each sampling point, record the point number, wind speed (Table 1), wind direction, sky conditions (Table 2), and temperature (degrees Fahrenheit). Prior to beginning the count, orient the field mapping card (Figure 2) to a fixed direction, record the direction in the box at the top of the count circle, and record the current time.

3. **Use Count-down Timer.** As soon as possible, begin the count, using the National Park Service (NPS)-issued count-down timer to keep track of time. Although the data will be transcribed to coding sheets later, the field mapping card is the only true record of what was detected during the survey. Even during the rush of a busy point count survey, remember to record data clearly and in a firm hand. When filling out the mapping cards make notations in a consistent manner and use the bird codes (Appendix A) and standardized symbols as defined on the field mapping card.

Count (record) All Birds and Squirrels. All birds and squirrels (see box below) seen and heard during the 10-minute sampling period should be counted and recorded on the NPS-issued field mapping card. Be sure to note in which minute birds are first encountered. This will require close attention to your count-down timer. For each bird detected, record on the field mapping card its 4-letter code followed by the minute it was first encountered (i.e., 9 for birds encountered during the first minute counting down to 0 for encounters during the last minute of the 10-minute survey period). See Figure 2 for a sample field mapping card. Remember that the crucial information is species identification, distance band, and time of first detection (in that order). No other information is required, although recording type of detection (i.e. visual versus calling or singing) may help you track the individuals. For flocks, estimate the number of individuals (don't try to mark each individual down). Birds that fly through or over the point count location and do not stay within the area of the point count do not meet the assumptions of distance or removal models. For these birds, record the species code in the top-right corner of the map (these observations are still valuable for telling us that the species is in the area).

Red squirrels, gray squirrels, and eastern chipmunks are known to be effective nest predators. We want to monitor their populations as well as those of forest birds. Follow the same recording procedures for these vocal mammals as you would for birds using these 4-letter codes:

- o RESQ - red squirrel
- o GRSQ - gray squirrel
- o CHIP - Eastern chipmunk

Table 1. Codes and descriptions for wind speeds (Beaufort Scale)[1]

Wind Speed Codes:

Code #	km/h	mph	Description
0	< 2	< 1	Smoke rises vertically
1	2 to 5	1 to 3	Wind direction shown by smoke drift
2	6 to 11	4 to 7	Wind felt on face; leaves rustle
3	12 to 20	8 to 12	Leaves, small twigs in constant motion; light flag extended
4	21 to 32	13 to 18	Small branches are moved
5	33 to 30	19 to 24	Small trees begin to sway

[1] These are the same codes used in the USGS Breeding Bird Survey. Acceptable conditions for counting birds include a wind speed of code 2 or less.

Table 2. Codes and descriptions for sky conditions[1]

Sky Conditions:

Code #	Description
0	Clear or a few clouds
1	Scattered clouds (partly cloudy)
2	Broken clouds or overcast
4	Fog
5	Drizzle or light rain
6	Rain
7	Snow
8	Showers

[1] These are the same codes used in the USGS Breeding Bird Survey. Acceptable conditions for counting birds include a sky condition of 5 or less (although fog should not interfere with visual identification of birds).

Figure 1. Example cover page of a field mapping card, including standardized symbols used to record observations made while conducting point counts.

FOREST BIRD MONITORING PROGRAM – FIELD CARD

PARK: MINUTE MAN NHP SITE: HARTWELL TAVERN

OBSERVER: BOB O. LINK DATE: 6 JUN 2009

Wind Speeds:	Wind Directions:	Sky Codes:
0 = calm, smoke rises vertically	N = north	0 = clear or a few clouds
1 = (1-3 mph) Light Air; rising smoke drifts	NE = northeast	1 = scattered clouds (partly
2 = (4-7 mph) Light Breeze; leaves rustle, can feel wind on face	E = east	cloudy)
3 = (8-12 mph) Gentle Breeze; leaves & twigs move	SE = southeast	2 = broken clouds or overcast
4 = (13-18 mph) Moderate Breeze; moves thin branches, raises loose paper	S = south	4 = fog
5 = (>18 mph) Fresh Breeze; trees sway	SW = southwest	5 = drizzle or light rain
ONLY CONDUCT SURVEYS WHEN 2 OR LESS	W = west	6 = rain – NO SURVEY
	NW = northwest	7 = snow – NO SURVEY
		8 = showers – NO SURVEY

MAPPING SYMBOLS

MAWA position of visually located magnolia warbler

 (MAWA) position of calling or singing magnolia warbler

MAWA ⟶ MAWA

Known change in position

MAWA - - → MAWA

Assumed change in position

If you use different symbols, describe them in the comments.

Survey Comments

POINT 5 HARD TO FIND ...
COULD USE MORE FLAGGING.

All codes on the field maps are correct, and data has been transcribed to the bird and mammal coding sheets. _____ (Signature)	**Mail to:** Steve Faccio VT Center for Ecostudies PO Box 420 Norwich, VT 05055

Figure 2. Example field mapping card

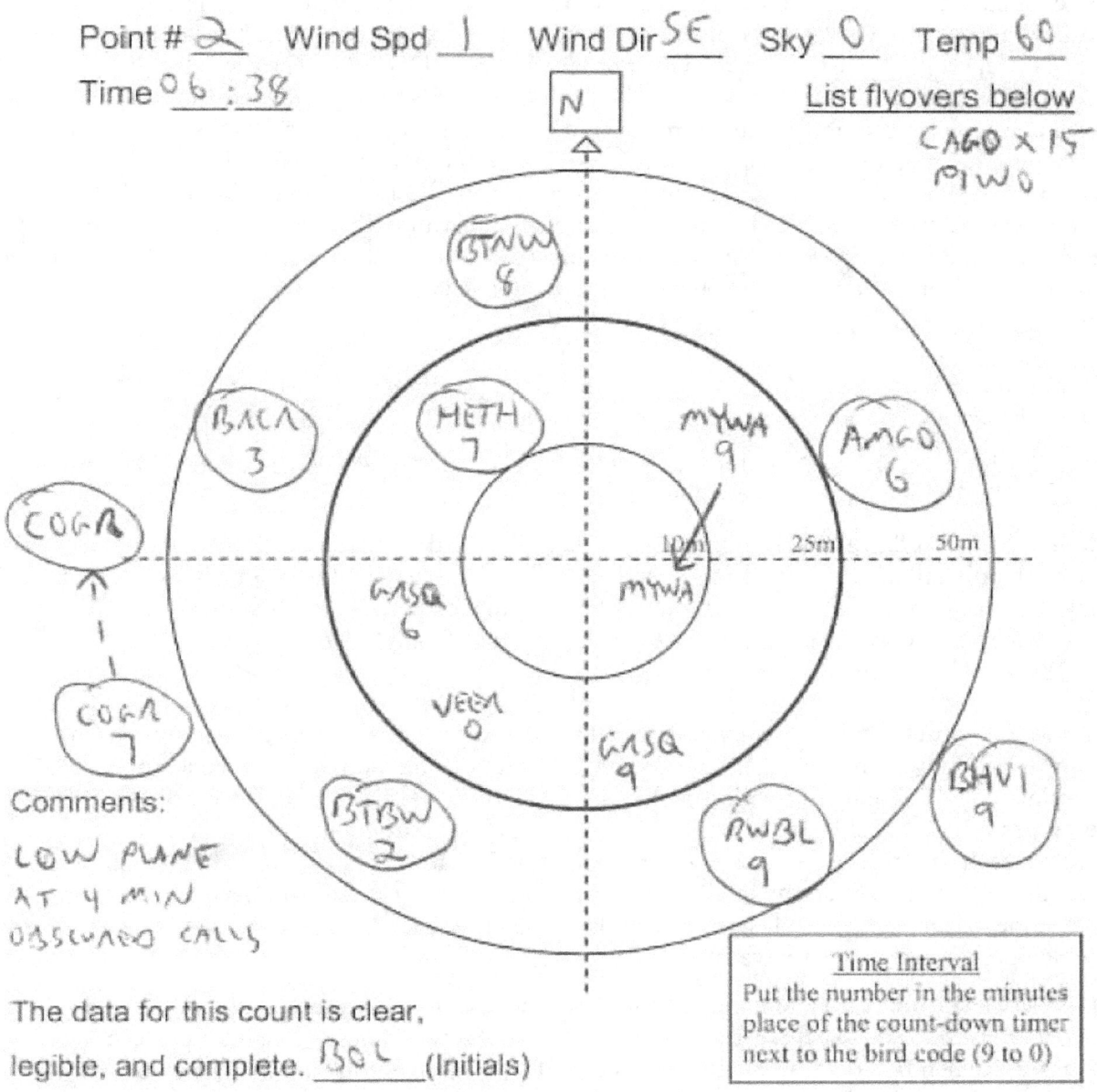

Point # 2   Wind Spd 1   Wind Dir SE   Sky 0   Temp 60
Time 06 : 38

List flyovers below
CAGO x 15
PIWO

Comments:
LOW PLANE
AT 4 MIN
OBSERVED CALLS

The data for this count is clear,
legible, and complete. BOL (Initials)

Time Interval
Put the number in the minutes
place of the count-down timer
next to the bird code (9 to 0)

4. **Map Observations.** Counting is done by mapping all observations (both visual and auditory) on the field mapping cards provided. Keep track of movements as best you can. Mapping (marking the location and noting movements) is the best way to reduce duplicate records. Mark birds on the field card in the appropriate distance band and approximate spatial location. The recorded distance should be the horizontal distance between the location a bird was <u>first detected</u> and the plot center. Imagine dropping a plumb-bob down from a bird's location and estimating its distance from the plot center. For species that occur in flocks, record the flock (e.g., species) and flock size in the appropriate distance band. There is no need to record each bird in a flock individually. Different symbols can be used to record the status of each bird observation (i.e. visual observation, calling or singing, etc., Figure 1 and Figure 2). Use standard species AOU codes to identify species observed (4-letter codes can be found in Appendix A, or downloaded at http://www.vtecostudies.org/FBMP/materials.html).

5. **Orientation.** Holding the field mapping card in a fixed position, spend part of the time facing in each of the cardinal directions in order to better detect birds.

6. **Count Individuals Once.** Do not record any birds believed to have been counted at previous stations. All birds should be counted only once.

7. **When to Stop.** At the end of 10 minutes, stop recording bird observations. Do not record any new birds seen or heard after the 10 minutes have passed. Before leaving the point, check over the field mapping card thoroughly to make sure it is complete and legible. Remember, this is the only record of what happened during the survey. Take the time to clarify anything illegible or out of the ordinary, and then initial the card.

8. **Sampling Frequency.** Each site should be sampled at least once during the breeding season, but one or two follow-up, replicate surveys within two weeks of the initial visit are encouraged. The exception to this is the three smallest parks (Saint-Gaudens NHS, Saugus Iron Works NHS, and Weir Farm NHS), which, due to their small sizes, can only accommodate a few point count locations each. In order to reduce between-year variability at these three parks, survey these sites twice annually, with surveys about 7-14 days apart. In order to reduce within- or between-site bias due to time of day, survey each study site in the same order each time (e.g., do not reverse the order in which point counts are surveyed).

9. **Data Transcription.** Bird and mammal data from the field mapping card(s) should be transcribed to separate data coding sheets (Figures 3 and 4) before they are entered into their respective databases. Remember, only transcribe the record of a bird or mammal the first time you saw or heard it. Each individual you encounter should only be recorded once on the summary data coding sheets. After completing each coding sheet, conduct a 100% check to look for transcription errors. If you need to correct information on the mapping card or data coding sheet (e.g., the wrong bird code was used), draw a single line through the incorrect data and then enter the correct data next to the original data, along with your initials and the date. Sign the data coding sheet indicating the 100% data transcription check has been completed. An overview of an observer's data management responsibilities can be found in Appendix C.

10. **Using the Online Database.** Once proofed, bird data recorded on data coding sheets should be entered into the USGS Bird Point Count Database (http://www.pwrc.usgs.gov/point/). Detailed instructions are provided in Appendix D. Verify each row of bird data as it is entered into the database and conduct a complete check of all data after finishing each data coding sheet.

Figure 3. Example of a Bird Data Coding Sheet

VERMONT CENTER ECOSTUDIES | Bird Data Coding Sheet – Landbird Monitoring Program

Park Name: MINUTE MAN NHP   Site Name: HARTWELL TAVERN

Observer: BOB O. LINK   Initials: BOL   Date: 6 JUN 2009

Did you observe small mammals during your survey? ☒ YES ☐ NO (If yes, fill out the Mammal Data Code Sheet)

Start Time	Point #	Species	Time Period	Obs Code	Distance Band	Flyovers/ # in flock	Start Time	Point #	Species	Time Period	Obs Code	Distance Band	Flyovers/ # in flock
0605	1	1. RBWO	9	C	3				26.				
	1	2. ETTI	9	C	1				27.				
	1	3. AMCR	6	C	4				28.				
	1	4. BCCH	1	C	2				29.				
0659	2	5. MYWA	9	1	2				30.				
	2	6. AMGO	6	C	3				31.				
	2	7. RWBL	9	C	3				32.				
	2	8. BHVI	9	C	4				33.				
	2	9. VEER	0	1	2				34.				
	2	10. BTAW	2	C	3				35.				
	2	11. COYE	7	C	4				36.				
	2	12. HETH	7	C	2				37.				
	2	13. BRCR	3	C	3				38.				
	2	14. BTNW	8	C	3				39.				
	2	15. CAGO	6	FL		X/15			40.				
	2	16. PIWO	2	FLC (BOL 6/JUN)		X			41.				
0762	3	17. ETTI	9	C	1				42.				
	3	18. AMRO	8	C	2				43.				
	3	19. OVEN	6	C	3				44.				
	3	20. WOTH	1	C	3				45.				
		21.							46.				
		22.							47.				
		23.							48.				
		24.							49.				
		25.							50.				

Time Period – Enter the time code (minute of the count when the bird was first observed). This is the digit displaying in the minutes place of your count-down timer (9 through 0; e.g. birds seen during the first minute of observation get a 9).

Codes used for bird occurrence – *Place the appropriate code from the list below in the "Obs Code" field in the table above*
Calling or singing = C   Individual seen = I   Flock = FL

Distance Band – *use the following codes to denote distance* – 1 = 0-10m   2 = 10-25m   3 = 25-50m   4 = >50m

Flyovers/# in flock – *place an X in column to denote flyovers, and/or a number to denote individuals observed in flocks.*

I proofed the transcription from the Field Mapping Cards: Signature:

I proofed data entered into database: Signature:

Page 1 of 1

Figure 4. Example of a Mammal Data Coding Sheet

VERMONT CENTER **ECOSTUDIES**
UNITING PEOPLE & SCIENCE FOR CONSERVATION

Mammal Data Coding Sheet – Landbird Monitoring Program

Park Name: MINUTE MAN NHP   Site Name: HARTWELL TAVERN

Observer: BOB O. LINK   Initials: BOL   Date: 6 JAN 2009

Point #	Species	Time Period	Obs Code	Distance Band		Point #	Species	Time Period	Obs Code	Distance Band
1	1. CHIP	3	1	2		26.				
2	2. GRSQ	9	1	2		27.				
2	3. GRSQ	6	1	2		28.				
3	4. CHIP	8	1	1		29.				
3	5. RESQ	9	C	3		30.				
	6.					31.				
	7.					32.				
	8.					33.				
	9.					34.				
	10.					35.				
	11.					36.				
	12.					37.				
	13.					38.				
	14.					39.				
	15.					40.				
	16.					41.				
	17.					42.				
	18.					43.				
	19.					44.				
	20.					45.				
	21.					46.				
	22.					47.				
	23.					48.				
	24.					49.				
	25.					50.				

Time Period – Enter the time code (minute of the count when the bird was first observed). This is the digit displaying in the minutes place of your count-down timer (9 through 0; e.g. birds seen during the first minute of observation get a 9).

Codes used for bird occurrence – *Place the appropriate code from the list below in the "Obs Code" field in the table above.* Calling = C   Individual seen = I

Distance Band – *use the following codes to denote distance* – 1 = 0-10m   2 = 10-25m   3 = 25-50m   4 = >50m

I proofed the transcription from the Field Mapping Cards: Signature: _____

Page 1 of 1

Sign the data coding sheet indicating that the 100% data entry check has been completed. Mammal data coding sheets are not entered in to the USGS database (its purpose is to store bird data only), but are sent on to the project manager after being proofed.

11. **Mail Data.** After bird data have been entered into the online database and proofed, mail the field mapping cards, the bird data coding sheets, and the mammal data coding sheets to:

> Forest Bird Monitoring Program
> Vermont Center for Ecostudies
> PO Box 420
> Norwich, VT 05055

Thanks for participating! For questions or additional information contact:

Steve Faccio
Vermont Center for Ecostudies
PO Box 420
Norwich, VT 05055
(802) 649-1431
E-mail: *sfaccio@vtecostudies.org*

Appendix A. Alphabetical List of Vermont FBMP Species and 4-letter codes. Mammal species listed in bold.

COMMON NAME	CODE	COMMON NAME	CODE
ALDER FLYCATCHER	ALFL	COOPER'S HAWK	COHA
AMERICAN CROW	AMCR	DOWNY WOODPECKER	DOWO
AMERICAN GOLDFINCH	AMGO	EASTERN BLUEBIRD	EABL
AMERICAN KESTREL	AMKE	**EASTERN CHIPMUNK**	**CHIP**
AMERICAN REDSTART	AMRE	EASTERN KINGBIRD	EAKI
AMERICAN ROBIN	AMRO	EASTERN MEADOWLARK	EAME
BALTIMORE ORIOLE	BAOR	EASTERN PHOEBE	EAPH
BANK SWALLOW	BANS	EASTERN SCREECH-OWL	EASO
BARN SWALLOW	BARS	EASTERN TOWHEE	EATO
BARRED OWL	BDOW	EASTERN TUFTED TITMOUSE	ETTI
BAY-BREASTED WARBLER	BBWA	EASTERN WOOD-PEWEE	EAWP
BELTED KINGFISHER	BEKI	EUROPEAN STARLING	EUST
BICKNELL'S THRUSH	BITH	EVENING GROSBEAK	EVGR
BLACK-AND-WHITE WARBLER	BAWW	FIELD SPARROW	FISP
BLACK-BACKED WOODPECKER	BBWO	FISH CROW	FICR
BLACK-BILLED CUCKOO	BBCU	GOLDEN-CROWNED KINGLET	GCKI
BLACKBURNIAN WARBLER	BLBW	GOLDEN-WINGED WARBLER	GWWA
BLACK-CAPPED CHICKADEE	BCCH	GRASSHOPPER SPARROW	GRSP
BLACKPOLL WARBLER	BLPW	GRAY CATBIRD	GRCA
BLACK-THROATED BLUE WARBLER	BTBW	GRAY JAY	GRAJ
BLACK-THROATED GREEN WARBLER	BTNW	**GRAY SQUIRREL**	**GRSQ**
BLUE JAY	BLJA	GREAT HORNED OWL	GHOW
BLUE-GRAY GNATCATCHER	BGGN	GREAT-CRESTED FLYCATCHER	GCFL
BLUE-WINGED WARBLER	BWWA	HAIRY WOODPECKER	HAWO
BOBOLINK	BOBO	HENSLOW'S SPARROW	HESP
BOREAL CHICKADEE	BOCH	HERMIT THRUSH	HETH
BROAD-WINGED HAWK	BWHA	HOODED WARBLER	HOWA
BROWN CREEPER	BRCR	HOUSE FINCH	HOFI
BROWN THRASHER	BRTH	HOUSE SPARROW	HOSP
BROWN-HEADED COWBIRD	BHCO	HOUSE WREN	HOWR
CANADA WARBLER	CAWA	INDIGO BUNTING	INBU
CAPE MAY WARBLER	CMWA	LEAST FLYCATCHER	LEFL
CAROLINA WREN	CARW	LINCOLN'S SPARROW	LISP
CEDAR WAXWING	CEDW	LOUISIANA WATERTHRUSH	LOWA
CERULEAN WARBLER	CERW	MAGNOLIA WARBLER	MAWA
CHESTNUT-SIDED WARBLER	CSWA	MARSH WREN	MAWR
CHIMNEY SWIFT	CHSW	MOURNING DOVE	MODO
CHIPPING SPARROW	CHSP	MOURNING WARBLER	MOWA
CLIFF SWALLOW	CLSW	MYRTLE WARBLER	MYWA
COMMON GRACKLE	COGR	NASHVILLE WARBLER	NAWA
COMMON NIGHTHAWK	CONI	NORTHERN CARDINAL	NOCA
COMMON RAVEN	CORA	NORTHERN GOSHAWK	NOGO
COMMON YELLOWTHROAT	COYE	NORTHERN HARRIER	NOHA
		NORTHERN MOCKINGBIRD	NOMO

NORTHERN PARULA	NOPA		WHITE-THROATED SPARROW	WTSP
NORTHERN ROUGH-WINGED SWALLOW	NRWS		WHITE-WINGED CROSSBILL	WWCR
			WILD TURKEY	WITU
NORTHERN SAW-WHET OWL	NSWO		WILLOW FLYCATCHER	WIFL
NORTHERN WATERTHRUSH	NOWA		WILSON'S WARBLER	WIWA
OLIVE-SIDED FLYCATCHER	OSFL		WINTER WREN	WIWR
ORCHARD ORIOLE	OROR		WOOD THRUSH	WOTH
OVENBIRD	OVEN		WORM-EATING WARBLER	WEWA
PHILADELPHIA VIREO	PHVI		YELLOW PALM WARBLER	YPWA
PILEATED WOODPECKER	PIWO		YELLOW WARBLER	YWAR
PINE SISKIN	PISI		YELLOW-BELLIED FLYCATCHER	YBFL
PINE WARBLER	PIWA		YELLOW-BELLIED SAPSUCKER	YBSA
PRAIRIE WARBLER	PRAW		YELLOW-BILLED CUCKOO	YBCU
PROTHONOTARY WARBLER	PROW		YELLOW-SHAFTED FLICKER	YSFL
PURPLE FINCH	PUFI		YELLOW-THROATED VIREO	YTVI
PURPLE MARTIN	PUMA			
RED CROSSBILL	RECR			
RED SQUIRREL	**RESQ**			
RED-BELLIED WOODPECKER	RBWO			
RED-BREASTED NUTHATCH	RBNU			
RED-EYED VIREO	REVI			
RED-HEADED WOODPECKER	RHWO			
RED-SHOULDERED HAWK	RSHA			
RED-TAILED HAWK	RTHA			
RED-WINGED BLACKBIRD	RWBL			
ROSE-BREASTED GROSBEAK	RBGR			
RUBY-CROWNED KINGLET	RCKI			
RUBY-THROATED HUMMINGBIRD	RTHU			
RUFFED GROUSE	RUGR			
RUSTY BLACKBIRD	RUBL			
SAVANNAH SPARROW	SAVS			
SCARLET TANAGER	SCTA			
SEDGE WREN	SEWR			
SHARP-SHINNED HAWK	SSHA			
SLATE-COLORED JUNCO	SCJU			
SOLITARY VIREO	SOVI			
SONG SPARROW	SOSP			
SWAINSON'S THRUSH	SWTH			
SWAMP SPARROW	SWSP			
TENNESSEE WARBLER	TEWA			
THREE-TOED WOODPECKER	TTWO			
TREE SWALLOW	TRES			
TURKEY VULTURE	TUVU			
VEERY	VEER			
VESPER SPARROW	VESP			
WARBLING VIREO	WAVI			
WHIP-POOR-WILL	WPWI			
WHITE-BREASTED NUTHATCH	WBNU			

Appendix B. Finding Your Way with Map and Compass

USGS Fact Sheet 035-01 (March 2001)

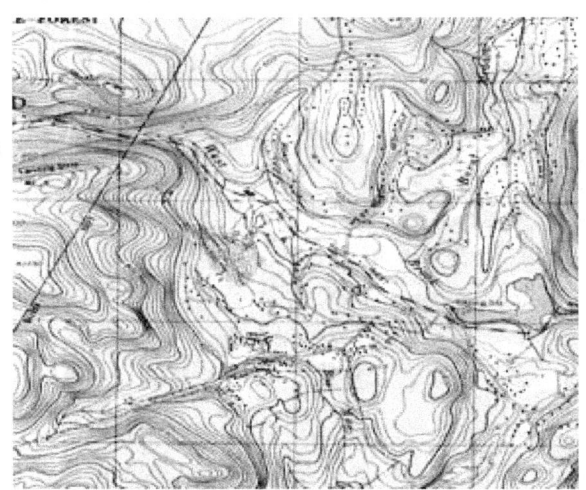

Part of a 7.5-minute topographic map at 1:24,000 scale.

A topographic map tells you where things are and how to get to them, whether you're hiking, biking, hunting, fishing, or just interested in the world around you. These maps describe the shape of the land. They define and locate natural and manmade features like woodlands, waterways, important buildings, and bridges. They show the distance between any two places, and they also show the direction from one point to another.

Distances and directions take a bit of figuring, but the topography and features of the land are easy to determine. The topography is shown by contours. These are imaginary lines that follow the ground surface at a constant elevation; they are usually printed in brown, in two thicknesses. The heavier lines are called index contours, and they are usually marked with numbers that give the height in feet or meters. The contour interval, a set difference in elevation between the brown lines, varies from map to map; its value is given in the margin of each map. Contour lines that are close together represent steep slopes.

Natural and manmade features are represented by colored areas and by a set of standard symbols on all U.S. Geological Survey (USGS) topographic maps. Woodlands, for instance, are shown in a green tint; waterways, in blue. Buildings may be shown on the map as black squares or outlines. Recent changes in an area may be shown by a purple overprint, a road may be printed in red or black solid or dashed lines, depending on its size and surface. A list of symbols is available from the Earth Science Information Center (ESIC) at http://ask.usgs.gov/sils_index.html.

From Near to Far: Distance

Maps are made to scale; that is, there is a direct relationship, a ratio, between a unit of measurement on the map and the actual distance that same unit of measurement represents on the ground. If, for instance, 1 inch on the map represents 1 mile (which converts to 63,360 inches) on the ground, the map's scale is 1:63,360. Below is a listing of the scales at which some of the more popular USGS maps are compiled.

A convenient way of representing map distance is by the use of a graphic scale bar. Most USGS topographic maps have scale bars in the map margin that represent distances on the map in miles, feet, and kilometers.

Appendix B. Finding Your Way with Map and Compass (continued).

The table below shows the corresponding area of coverage for each scale and the linear distance that each scale represents in inches and centimeters.

Map Name Series	Scale	1 inch represents	1 centimeter represents	Map area (approximate square miles)
Puerto Rico 7.5 minute	1:20,000	1,667 feet	200 meters	71
7.5-minute	1:24,000	2,000 feet	240 meters	40 to 70
7.5- by 15-minute	1:25,000	2,083 feet	250 meters (about)	98 to 140
Alaska	1:63,360	1 mile	634 meters (about)	207 to 281
Intermediate	1:50,000	0.8 mile	500 meters (about)	County
Intermediate	1:100,000	1.6 mile	1 kilometer (about)	1,568 to 2,240
United States	1:250,000	4 miles	2. 5 kilometers (about)	4,580 to 8,669

From Here to There: Determining Direction

To determine the direction, or bearing, from one point to another, you need a compass as well as a map. Most compasses are marked with the four cardinal points—north, east, south, and west—but some are marked additionally with the number of degrees in a circle (360: north is 0 or 360, east is 90, south is 180, and west is 270). Both kinds are easy to use with a little practice. The illustrations on the next page show how to read direction on a map.

One thing to remember is that a compass does not really point to true north, except by coincidence in some areas. The compass needle is attracted by magnetic force, which varies in different parts of the world and is constantly changing. When you read north on a compass, you're really reading the direction of the magnetic north pole. A diagram in the map margin will show the difference (declination) at the center of the map between compass north (magnetic north indicated by the MN symbol) and true north (polar north indicated by the "star" symbol). This diagram also provides the declination between true north and the orientation of the Universal Transverse Mercator (UTM) grid north (indicated by the GN symbol). The declination diagram is only representational, and true values of the angles of declination should be taken from the numbers provided rather than from the directional lines. Because the magnetic declination is computed at the time the map is made, and because the position of magnetic north is constantly changing, the declination factor provided on any given map may not be current. To obtain current and historical magnetic declination information for any place in the United States, contact:

National Geomagnetic Information Center
Phone: 303-273-8486
E-mail: jcaldwell@usgs.gov
Web site: geomag.usgs.gov.
or
National Geophysical Data Center
Phone: 303-497-6826
E-mail: info@ngdc.noaa.gov
Web site: www.ngdc.noaa.gov/ or www.ngdc.noaa.gov/seg/potfld/geomag.shtml.

Appendix B. Finding Your Way with Map and Compass (continued).

Taking a compass bearing from a map:

1. Draw a straight line on the map passing through your location and your destination and extending across any one of the map borders.
2. Center the compass where your drawn line intersects the map border, align the compass axis N-S or E-W with the border line, and read on the compass circle the true bearing of your drawn line. Be careful to get the bearing in the correct sense because a straight line will have two values 180° apart. Remember north is 0, east is 90, and so on.
3. To use this bearing, you must compensate for magnetic declination. If the MN arrow on the map magnetic declination diagram is to the right of the true north line, subtract the MN value. If the arrow is to the left of the line, add the value. Then, standing on your location on the ground, set the compass so that "zero degrees or North" aligns with the magnetic north needle, read the magnetic bearing that you have determined by this procedure, and head off in the direction of this bearing to reach your destination.

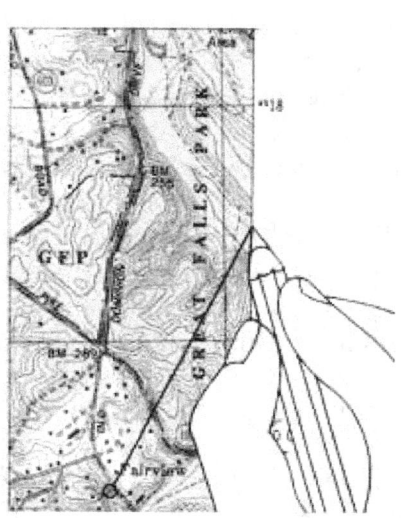   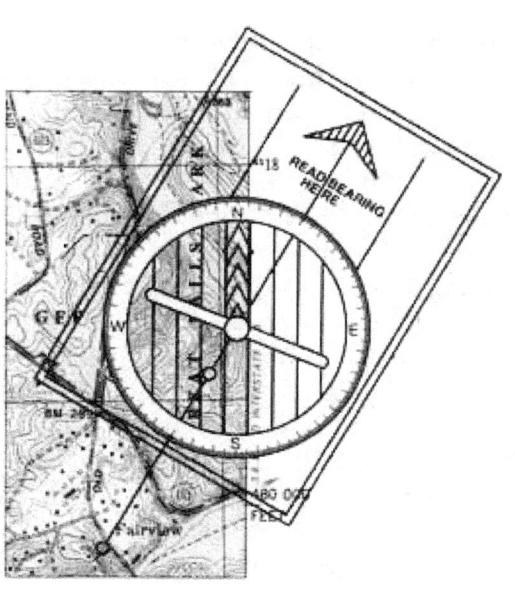

(1) Drawing a straight line over the map edge   (2) Reading the compass on the map

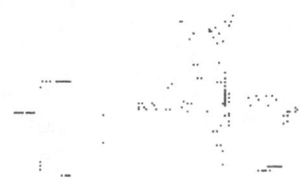

(3) Using the magnetic declination diagrams

16

Appendix B. Finding Your Way with Map and Compass (continued).

NOTE: Unless otherwise noted, all compass bearings that are used as part of NETN forest bird monitoring point counts reference to magnetic north. As such, compensating for magnetic declination is not required.

A Word of Caution

Compass readings are also affected by the presence of iron and steel objects. Be sure to look out for—and stay away from—pocket knives, belt buckles, railroad tracks, trucks, electrical lines, and so forth when using a compass in the field.

Information

For information on these and other USGS products and services, call 1-888-ASK-USGS, or visit the general interest publications Web site on mapping, geography, and related topics at erg.usgs.gov/isb/pubs/pubslists/.

For additional information, visit the ask.usgs.gov web site or the USGS home page at www.usgs.gov.

Appendix C. Flow chart of volunteer observers' data management responsibilities.

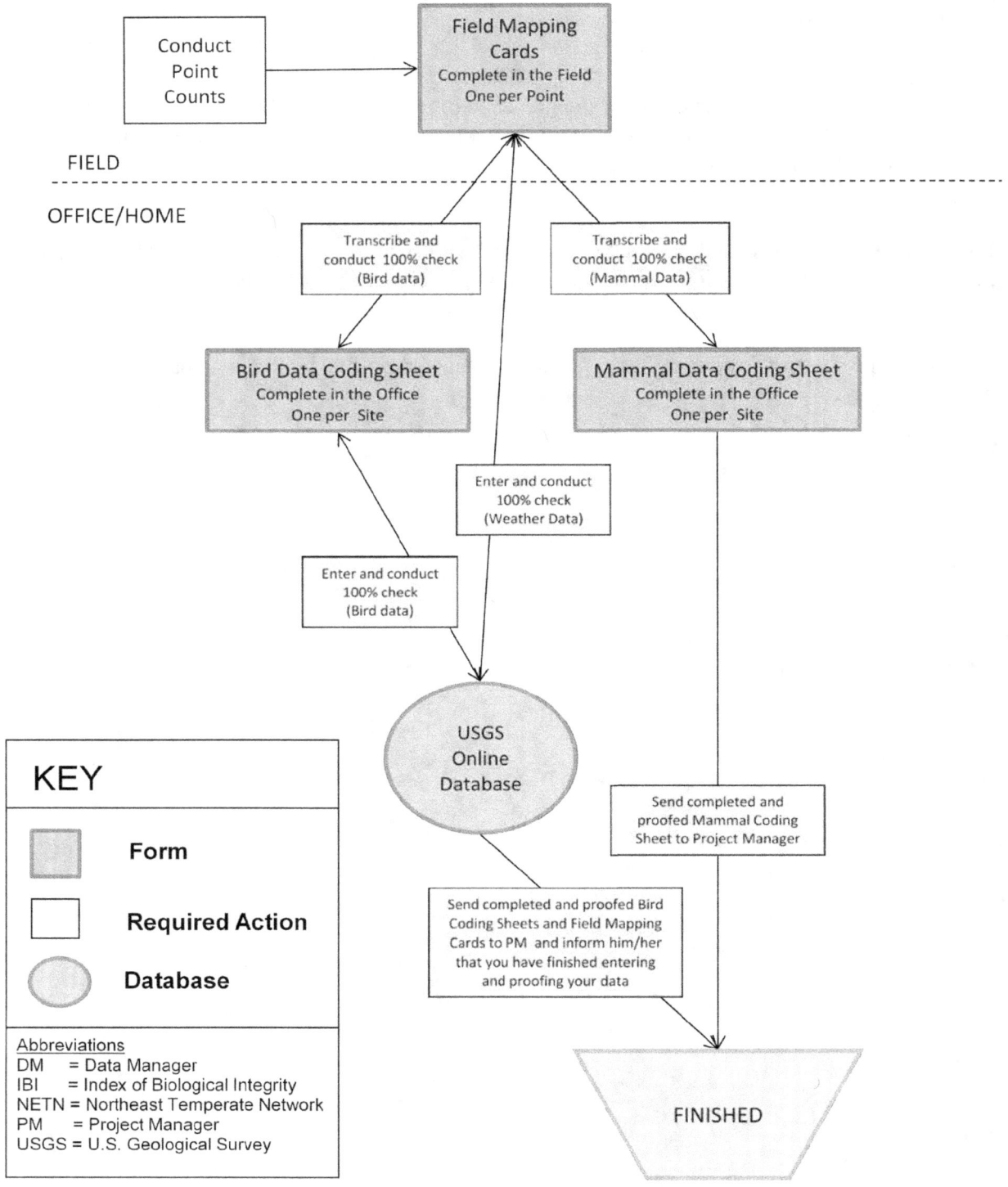

Appendix D. Instructions for entering data online.

Online Data Entry Instructions for the USGS Avian Point Count Database

These instructions describe the steps required to enter data found on the Bird Data Coding Sheets into the online Bird Point Count Database. The database is designed to only store bird data. Mammal data (squirrels and chipmunks) collected during point count surveys should be transcribed to a Mammal Data Coding Sheet, checked for transcription errors, and sent to the Program Manager.

1) Before entering bird data into the online database, please verify that the bird coding data sheet has been checked against the original field mapping cards to catch any transcription errors. If this has been completed the verification statement on the bottom of the coding sheet will have been signed and you can proceed to enter the data into the online database. If the statement hasn't been signed, please conduct a 100% check of the data before proceeding.

2) Navigate your web browser to the Bird Point Count Database website http://www.pwrc.usgs.gov/point/. On the right side of the screen, sign-in using the username and password that you should have received via a separate email from Mark Wimer at the Bird Point Count Database. If you cannot locate your sign-in info, click on "Forgot Password" located below the sign-in section of the webpage. If you did not receive your sign-in info, contact the Project Manager and he/she will get it to you ASAP.

3) Once you have successfully signed-in, click on **"Bird Surveys"** under **MANAGE / ENTER DATA**.

4) Then, on the next screen, click on **"Add New Bird Survey"** on the right side of the screen.

5) On the next screen, first select the study that you are participating in (in this case, "National Park surveys"), then select the name of your study site from the second drop down menu. Select the point count number for which you want to enter data and proceed down the list filling in the necessary info. After **"Weather Conditions,"** select, **"Enter Species Using Blank Form** (for now, ignore the last box that says, **"Or (faster) enter codes here:")**. Click **"NEXT."** Because this is a bird database, squirrels and chipmunks are not included in the species list on the next page. Squirrel and chipmunk data should be entered onto a mammal data coding sheet and mailed to the project manager (Steve Faccio).

6) Now you can enter data for the first point by typing in the species code in the left-hand box. An alphabetical list of species will appear as you begin typing – you can either choose the highlighted species name from the list or simply type in the correct four-letter code (please note that squirrels and chipmunk are not included in this list, so for now do not enter any that you recorded). Then from the three dropdown menus select the appropriate Time Period, ObsCode, and Distance Band. For flyovers, you can enter "not recorded" for Time Period, ObsCode, and Distance. If you get to the bottom of the screen

Appendix D. Instructions for entering data online (continued).

and still have more birds to enter, click on "**Add Row**" and continue until you have entered all the individuals from the first point. Then select "**SAVE**".

7) On the next screen, you can select "**Repeat Values**" to the right of the Point Number dropdown to fill-in the previous Survey data. Change the **point number** and **start-time**, and change the other values (if needed) to reflect the weather conditions during the count.

8) Continue until you have entered all the data. When completed, click on "**sign out**" in the upper right hand corner of the screen.

9) Send an email to *sfaccio@vtecostudies.org* indicating that you have completed the data entry.

10) Mail your completed field cards and data coding sheets to the address listed on the field cards and on page 6 of this manual.

Appendix E. Checklist of volunteer tasks.

Field Season Completion Checklist

The checklist below is an important part of our quality control procedures. Please initial and date each task as it is completed, and return this sheet once data entry is complete (by 15 August).

Name_____   Park_____

	Initials	Date	TASK	When to Accomplish
1			Read/review Volunteer Training Manual	Mid- to late-May
2			Practice distance estimation as outlined in Volunteer Training Manual	Mid- to late-May
3			Brush-up on bird songs in the field or with recordings	Mid- to late-May
4			Conduct first field survey (last week of May surveys are acceptable at MORR and WEFA)	1-15 June
5			Conduct second field survey (optional at some parks)	15-30 June
6			Transcribe data from Field Mapping Cards onto Data Coding Sheets	Within 1 day of conducting field survey
7			Make photocopies of Field Mapping Cards and Data Coding Sheets and mail originals to VCE (address below). Retain copies for use in data entry.	Within 3 days of conducting last field survey.
8			Enter field data into Bird Point Count Database and return this sheet to VCE (address below).	No later than 15 August
9			Total up volunteer hours contributed to project this season and enter below.	No later than 15 August
10			Complete and sign NPS *Agreement for Individual Voluntary Services* form and return to VCE with this sheet.	No later than 15 August
TOTAL VOLUNTEER HOURS:				
Comments:				

Mail to: Steve Faccio
VCE
PO Box 420
Norwich, VT 05055

Revision History Log

Version	Date	Revised By	Changes	Justification
1.00	January 2006	Steve Faccio	Version associated with the Recruiting and Training Volunteer Observers SOP used beginning with the 2006 field season.	
1.01	April 2006	Brian Mitchell	Change to Recruiting and Training Volunteer Observers SOP	
1.02	December 2008	Steve Faccio Brian Mitchell	Recruiting and Training Volunteer Observers SOP	
1.03	February 2009	Steve Faccio	Volunteer Training Manual added as Appendix 2.2 of Recruiting and Training Volunteer Observers SOP	
1.04	August 2009	Sarah Lupis	Formatting, minor editorial changes.	
2.00	February 2010	Adam Kozlowski and Brian Mitchell	Significant revision to Volunteer Training Manual to reflect streamlined field procedures and updated data management procedures. Updated survey procedures and added mammal data coding sheet. Added volunteer data management responsibilities appendix.	Changes to reflect efforts to simplify field data collection and improve data management procedures.
2.01	March 2010	Steve Faccio	Minor editorial changes during review	
2.02	April 2010	Ed Sharron	Formatting, minor editorial changes.	

Northeast Temperate Network
Inventory & Monitoring Program

EXPERIENCE YOUR AMERICA ™